101 QUIZZES

for

BRIDES&
GROOMS

Take These Tests to Discover Your
*Wedding Personality & Customize
Your Big Day Together*

NATASHA BURTON

A adamsmedia
AVON, MASSACHUSETTS

DEDICATION

For my handsome groom, Greg St. Clair,
and our future bride-to-be.

Published by
Adams Media, a division of F+W Media, Inc.
57 Littlefield Street, Avon, MA 02322. U.S.A.
www.adamsmedia.com

ISBN 10: 1-4405-9532-1
ISBN 13: 978-1-4405-9532-5

Printed in the United States of America.

10   9   8   7   6   5   4   3   2   1

Cover design by Alexandra Artiano.
Cover images © iStockphoto.com/DavidGoh; OliaFedorovsky;
Roberto Scandola/123RF.

This book is available at quantity discounts for bulk purchases.
For information, please call 1-800-289-0963.

CONTENTS

ACKNOWLEDGMENTS

Thank you to the fabulous team at Adams Media, particularly Brendan O'Neill, Laura Daly, and Christine Dore, for the continued support of my writing and for publishing this book. I'd also like to thank my wonderful former agent Elizabeth Evans and my lovely new agent Laura Biagi, along with everyone else at JVNLA, for making my career possible.

Even though I worked at *HuffPost Weddings* and have written about weddings for years, the greatest source of wedding-planning knowledge has come from planning my own wedding in 2014. (You learn by doing, after all, right?) This book is a result of everything I wish I had thought of, or that I wish someone had told me to think of, as I was coordinating my wedding with my now husband. (My mom was an instrumental part of the journey, too: Thank you, Mom, for tirelessly talking about which plates to rent and how to get the flowers I envisioned just right. You made the day beautiful and unforgettable!)

Postwedding, I was so inspired by everything I learned that I cofounded a boutique event-planning company, Swoon California, with my best friend, Jennifer Arreguin. Thank you, Jenn, for being my business partner and sister-by-choice.

And, to save the best for last, thank you to my wonderful husband (and total babe) Greg St. Clair. Not only for dealing with the craziness that came with planning our wedding, but for always encouraging me to follow my passions—even if that now means perpetual, endless wedding planning because I've decided to do it for other people. I love you. (And get ready to plan another wedding in thirty or so years when it's our daughter's turn to walk down the aisle!)

INTRODUCTION

Congratulations on your engagement! Now that you've taken the next step in your relationship, it's time to start planning the event at which you'll tie the knot—your wedding.

Whether you've dreamed of this moment since childhood or haven't really given it much thought, coordinating your nuptials is an exciting time for both of you. And it can be a great opportunity to get even closer as a couple as you imagine your ideal wedding, practice your compromising skills, and work together to create a monumental celebration of your love. (And throw one kick-ass party, of course!)

While wedding planning is certainly fun, it can also be pretty overwhelming: With the advent of Pinterest—and the litany of wedding-related blogs—it's easy to feel intimidated by endless lists of "must-haves" and expectations for Instagram-worthy décor. That's where this book comes in: Taking these quizzes will help you navigate this special time in your relationship and create a personalized wedding-planning roadmap based on *your* wants and desires, not what's trendy, what's traditional, or what your parents expect, for that matter.

Some of the questions this book will help you answer are:

- Where and when should we celebrate our marriage?
- Who should we invite—and not invite?
- How can our wedding-day attire reflect our personal style?

- What décor details will showcase our personalities?
- How much do we *really* want to spend on things like napkins and chairs?
- . . . and many, many more!

Because this book is designed to cover a wide range of possibilities, tastes, and types of weddings, not every quiz will perfectly fit your big-day expectations. And that's okay! What each quiz will do is encourage you to explore what really matters, and what *so* doesn't, when it comes to your wedding so you can plan an event that truly captures who you two are as a couple.

How to Use This Book

This book is designed to guide you through the dreaming and conceptualizing part of the planning process. To get the most out of the quizzes, it's best to take them in order so you can define your overall wedding style first, then address the details. This way, everything will just fall right into place.

By clearly defining your vision for each facet of your big day—starting with the big picture—you'll be well equipped to go on to the next stage of planning, which involves hiring your vendors, selecting everything from your menu to the décor, and determining the actual logistics of your celebration. Answering these quizzes before doing the nitty-gritty planning will make the entire journey smoother and more fun, as well as ensure that your wedding really reflects your relationship.

While some quizzes may be directed toward "brides" or "grooms" specifically, this book was written with all couples in mind, from different-sex couples to same-sex couples to gender-queer couples. The bride and groom designations are merely meant to serve as a framework for you to adapt as needed: For instance, if you're a same-sex couple of two brides, you'll both just take the quizzes geared toward brides. Or if you're a bride who'd prefer to wear a suit and sneakers on her wedding day, you might find more inspiration in the quizzes geared toward grooms.

The bottom line is this: Use this book how it works best for *you* and your ideal celebration. After all, every couple—every person!—is unique. These quizzes are meant to open up your wedding-day possibilities, not restrict them. If you find that the two of you disagree on an issue, ask yourselves how important the topic is, and then brainstorm to see if you can reach a compromise that works for both of you.

About the Quizzes

There are a variety of quiz types in this book to inspire your wedding-planning journey and encourage you to dream big when it comes to designing your ultimate celebration. Each quiz also includes additional context to provide extra insight about a given part of the planning process. Here are the various types you'll find:

Pop Quiz

Just like when you were in school, these quizzes are meant to be filled in quickly so your gut feelings and wants will be revealed.

Brainstorm

These list-style quizzes serve as idea starters for you to explore the endless possibilities while wedding planning. As you take these, feel free to jot down additional ideas of your own at the end of each list.

This or That?

By pitting two ideas against each other, these quizzes help you determine where your loyalty lies for a given decision or detail.

Checklist

These quizzes ask you to check off items that appeal to you so you can get a clearer picture of what you might want or need for a particular facet of your wedding.

True or False and Me/You

Giving you two choices, much like This or That?, these quiz types will help you make decisions and voice how you really feel about certain planning tasks and wedding details.

Multiple Choice

These quizzes help you define your wants and needs by providing various options and allowing you to select what appeals to you most.

Open-Ended

Many quizzes consist of a series of open-ended questions that allow you to think freely and elaborate on a particular part of the planning process.

Let's Start Planning!

Ready to dive into the world of venue picking, bridal parties, and tablescapes? Turn the page and let the wedding planning begin!

1

What's Your Wedding's Personality?

What Are Our Wedding-Planning Expectations?

These questions will help you figure out how each of you envisions the wedding-planning process.

		ME	YOU
1.	It's going to be fun.	ME ❏	YOU ❏
2.	It's going to be a lot of work.	ME ❏	YOU ❏
3.	It's going to be stressful.	ME ❏	YOU ❏
4.	We're going to see eye-to-eye on most things.	ME ❏	YOU ❏
5.	We're going to need to learn the art of compromise.	ME ❏	YOU ❏
6.	We should talk about planning every day.	ME ❏	YOU ❏
7.	We should designate a certain day of the week for planning.	ME ❏	YOU ❏
8.	We should try to plan everything ASAP to get it done.	ME ❏	YOU ❏
9.	We should plan things in stages to keep from getting overwhelmed.	ME ❏	YOU ❏
10.	We should plan most things together.	ME ❏	YOU ❏
11.	We should involve our parents/whoever is paying in our decision-making.	ME ❏	YOU ❏
12.	We should divide and conquer our to-do list.	ME ❏	YOU ❏

What Are Our Wedding-Planning Personalities?

Your everyday planning personalities will likely translate into your wedding-planning personalities. Answer these questions about how you typically get things done.

1. I like to make lists and will use them to stay on task. **ME** ❏ | **YOU** ❏

2. I like the idea of tackling our to-dos once a month in one long session. **ME** ❏ | **YOU** ❏

3. I like the idea of planning a little bit each day. **ME** ❏ | **YOU** ❏

4. I'm type A all the way and really good at planning things. **ME** ❏ | **YOU** ❏

5. I'm a more laid-back planner. **ME** ❏ | **YOU** ❏

6. I'm not a planner and tend to be disorganized. **ME** ❏ | **YOU** ❏

7. I like planning things over e-mail and using online tools like Pinterest and Google Docs. **ME** ❏ | **YOU** ❏

8. I like planning by talking and making vision boards using real photos and magazine tear-outs. **ME** ❏ | **YOU** ❏

9. I want to have a clear schedule of when things should get done. **ME** ❏ | **YOU** ❏

10. I want to be more spontaneous with planning—we do things when we do them. **ME** ❏ | **YOU** ❏

11. I want to eliminate as many to-dos as possible by *really* thinking about what we actually need to do, have, and include at our wedding. **ME** ❏ | **YOU** ❏

12. I want to plan the wedding with our guests in mind, first and foremost. **ME** ❏ | **YOU** ❏

13. I want to plan the wedding with our wants and needs in mind, first and foremost. **ME** ❏ | **YOU** ❏

What Planning Tasks Are We Each Most Excited About?

Each of you should select three things you're most looking forward to, which can help you determine who should handle what if you decide to split up planning tasks.

- ❏ Deciding on the colors, décor, flowers, and general style of the event
- ❏ Picking out a band or DJ
- ❏ Choosing the food
- ❏ Selecting what to stock in the bar
- ❏ Deciding on favors to give our guests
- ❏ Designing a wedding website
- ❏ Picking out a cool mode of transportation for us and/or our guests
- ❏ Choosing readings for the ceremony
- ❏ Picking out gifts for parents and attendants
- ❏ Selecting what we're going to wear

What's Our Plan of Action When Wedding Planning Gets Overwhelming?

Even the most laid-back people can feel like they need a break from wedding planning. Anticipating that ahead of time will save you stress and unnecessary spats.

1. What's our wedding-planning mantra, i.e. the one thing we truly believe matters when it comes to our big day?

   _____

   _____

2. What are three things we can do to relax if we start getting stressed?

   _____

   _____

3. If we decide we need a break from planning, what should that look like and how long should it last?

   _____

   _____

4. If we have trouble making a decision, what should be the final decider? (Flip a coin? Ask a friend? You choose!)

   _____

   _____

5. Designate a funny word or phrase we can say if we don't want to talk about the wedding anymore that moment, or that day:

   _____

   _____

6. What should we do if one of us really wants or cares about a certain detail and the other person doesn't?

_____

_____

7. What's the best way to (gently) let the other person know when he or she has gone off the deep end while planning?

_____

_____

8. How should we deal with the not-so-fun planning tasks that start stressing us out? (Delegate to a parent? Make a quick decision? Put on hold for another day?)

_____

_____

9. How can we remind each other to not sweat the small stuff while planning?

_____

_____

10. When we look back on our wedding years from now, what's the one thing we want to be able to remember or say about our big day?

_____

_____

How Much Planning Do We Want to Do Ourselves?

Use this quiz to determine if you should hire a wedding planner, a day-of coordinator, or someone who can help with event design.

1. We want someone who can take all of our ideas and execute them for us. **TRUE** ❑ | **FALSE** ❑

2. We're not great at delegating—having someone else handle things may be stressful. **TRUE** ❑ | **FALSE** ❑

3. We really just need someone to manage the event on the day of. **TRUE** ❑ | **FALSE** ❑

4. We'd prefer to have a professional introduce us to wedding vendors. **TRUE** ❑ | **FALSE** ❑

5. We'll need help deciding on a venue. **TRUE** ❑ | **FALSE** ❑

6. We'll need assistance bringing our design ideas to life. **TRUE** ❑ | **FALSE** ❑

7. We like the idea of doing all the legwork ourselves but being able to hand things over to a professional on the big day. **TRUE** ❑ | **FALSE** ❑

8. We already have some vendors in mind so we don't need help finding our wedding dream team. **TRUE** ❑ | **FALSE** ❑

9. We want someone who can accompany us to vendor meetings and tastings to guide our decisions. **TRUE** ❑ | **FALSE** ❑

10. We don't have a lot of time in our schedules for planning, so having someone on hand to work on logistics would be ideal. **TRUE** ❑ | **FALSE** ❑

Our Ideal Wedding Planner/Coordinator

Use the following quiz to check off the personality traits you'd want to see in the person who will be at the helm on your big day.

❑ Talkative and enthusiastic

❑ Reserved and more quiet

❑ Offers lots of suggestions upfront

❑ Gives us honest feedback about our ideas and plans

❑ Encourages our vision without making comments

❑ Brings up considerations we haven't thought of

❑ Super organized

❑ Goes with the flow and laid-back

❑ Patient and happy to explain things

❑ Good at problem-solving

❑ Able to work with our budget

❑ Passionate about what he/she does

Where Can We Look for Wedding Inspiration?

Before you decide on your wedding wants, first turn to various resources for ideas. (Not all will apply or appeal to you, so just circle which ones suit you best!)

1. Pinterest
2. Lover.ly
3. Wedding blogs
4. Wedding magazines
5. Celebrity wedding photos/articles
6. Art and design blogs/books
7. Runway shows
8. Entertaining magazines and blogs
9. Window displays in favorite stores
10. Photos of cities, locations, and spaces we love—from favorite restaurants to a local park
11. Our lifestyle—our home décor and what we like to do for fun
12. Photos of previous parties we've thrown and vacations we've taken together
13. Memories from friends' and family members' weddings
14. Conversations with friends and family members about their wedding priorities and experiences (for insider insight!)

Our Favorite Things

Fill out this quiz to get ideas on how you can bring some unique-to-you details into your big day and really make the celebration personal.

1. Our favorite TV show(s):

   _____

   _____

2. Our favorite movie(s):

   _____

   _____

3. Our favorite recipe to make together or for family and friends:

   _____

   _____

4. Our favorite holiday:

   _____

   _____

5. Our favorite things to do together:

   _____

   _____

6. Our favorite sports teams:

   _____

   _____

7. Our favorite games and activities:

   _____

   _____

8. Our favorite Halloween costume:

_____

_____

9. Our favorite cities/countries/places:

_____

_____

10. Our favorite weekend plans:

_____

_____

What Themes Inspire Us?

Check out these common—and out-of-the-box—wedding themes to see if any fit your style. Circle as many as you like.

1. Costume party
2. White party (everyone wears white)
3. Masquerade ball
4. *Great Gatsby*–inspired/1920s
5. Holiday—Christmas, Halloween, etc.
6. Fairy tale
7. Sports/athletic
8. School (our alma maters)
9. Carnival
10. Music festival
11. Travel
12. Literary
13. Geeky

Personalizing Our Wedding

Fill out this quiz to get ideas on how you can bring in some specific-to-your-relationship details into your celebration to really make it meaningful.

1. Our relationship can be summed up in these three words:

_____

_____

2. Our friends describe us as the couple who:

_____

_____

3. How we met:

_____

_____

4. Where we met:

_____

_____

5. Our shared philosophies on love:

_____

_____

6. Our rituals or things we always do together:

_____

_____

7. Memorable trips we've taken or places we've visited:

_____

_____

8. Ways we've celebrated our anniversaries or other milestones:

_____

_____

9. How we want others to see our relationship:

_____

_____

10. Where we see ourselves in ten years:

_____

_____

How Formal, or Not, Should Our Wedding Be?

Weddings can run the gamut on the formality scale, from flip-flops on the beach to full-on black tie. Where will yours fall?

1. When we're invited to a black-tie wedding, our first thought is:
   a. Finally! Now we can dress up!
   b. Fun! But . . . eek! What do we wear?!
   c. Groan . . .

2. Our ideal wedding décor is:
   a. Tons and tons of flowers with candles and pretty linens
   b. Photos of the two of us with some cool lanterns
   c. We don't really care all that much about décor

3. Our ideal wedding venue is:
   a. A gorgeous hotel
   b. A rustic barn or private home
   c. Our backyard

4. When we imagine our wedding food, we think:
   a. Four-course meal
   b. Family-style or buffet
   c. Food trucks

5. Our wedding attire must include:
   a. A tiara and a bow tie
   b. A flowy dress and a suit
   c. Anything we don't have to wear fancy shoes with

6. Our general style, in life, is:
   a. Sophisticated
   b. Down-to-earth
   c. Casual

7. The thought of our friends and family members in nice suits and dresses is:
   a. Not anything new
   b. A nice change from the everyday
   c. Shocking

8. At our wedding, we want to:
   a. Feel extra fancy
   b. Be comfortable
   c. Just hang out

9. We tend to get dressed up:
   a. Whenever we have an excuse to (and sometimes we create an excuse ourselves!)
   b. When the occasion calls for it
   c. Almost never

10. We definitely don't want our wedding to feel:
   a. Casual
   b. Too formal
   c. Stuffy

What Are Our Wedding Priorities?

From the following list, circle three things that are absolute must-haves for your wedding.

1. A beautiful or interesting venue
2. A unique menu
3. A convenient location
4. A packed dance floor
5. Amazing entertainment
6. Really, really good food
7. Personalized DIY touches
8. Gorgeous flowers
9. A big guest list
10. Somewhat predictable weather
11. Special details or elements we haven't seen at any other wedding
12. A meaningful ceremony
13. Getting married in a particular city, state, or country
14. Delicious dessert
15. An unforgettable entrance or grand exit
16. A private or secluded venue

Narrowing Down Our Ideal Wedding Wants

Sometimes you can't have *everything* you want. Use this quiz to help you prioritize what's most important to you two.

1. Bigger guest list -OR- better food?
2. Awesome location -OR- more convenient venue? Both!
3. Pricier photographer -OR- more flowers?
4. All-inclusive venue -OR- having to hire more vendors?
5. Off-season wedding -OR- getting hitched in the spring or summer?
6. Get married ASAP -OR- have more lead time to plan?
7. Designer wedding gown -OR- honeymoon shopping fund? Down payment on house!
8. Religious service -OR- super-personalized ceremony?
9. Band -OR- DJ?
10. Honeymoon right after wedding day -OR- postwedding brunch? Mini moon!
11. Buying/renting décor -OR- doing DIY projects? Both?
12. Live ceremony music -OR- recorded? No pref
13. Hiring a full-service planner -OR- a day-of coordinator?

Best of the Best Weddings We've Attended

There's nothing wrong with getting inspiration from your friends and families! Think back to some events you've gone to and list some of your favorite aspects.

1. Most fun overall:

   _____

2. Coolest location:

   _____

3. Best food:

   _____

4. Most unique:

   _____

5. Best party/atmosphere:

   _____

6. Best personalized details:

   _____

7. Best guest experience:

   _____

8. Best entertainment:

   _____

9. Best décor:

   _____

10. Most romantic:

   _____

What Words Describe Your Ideal Wedding Vibe?

Circle all the adjectives that you want to sum up your wedding.

1. Fun
2. Laid-back
3. Traditional
4. Unique
5. Intimate
6. Romantic
7. Exciting
8. Joyful
9. Formal
10. Emotional
11. Wild
12. Casual

What Words Describe Your Ideal Wedding Décor?

Circle all the adjectives that describe the look and feel you're going for with the décor.

1. Fancy
2. Rustic
3. Elegant
4. Whimsical
5. Colorful
6. Classic
7. Modern
8. Shabby chic
9. Glam
10. Artsy
11. Beachy
12. Preppy
13. Ornate
14. Bespoke
15. Simple
16. Stylish
17. Tropical

What Colors Are You Drawn To?

Circle your top five favorite colors.

1. Whites and creams
2. Blues
3. Neons and bright hues
4. Pinks
5. Greens
6. Black
7. Gray
8. Yellows
9. Corals
10. Oranges
11. Purples
12. Pastels

What Textures Are You Drawn To?

Circle your top five favorite textures.

1. Metallics—like gold, silver, or copper
2. Glitter
3. Stone—like brick or concrete
4. Metal—like stainless steel or brass
5. Grass
6. Earth—like dirt or hiking trails
7. Sand
8. Velvet and other lush fabrics
9. Tulle and other light fabrics
10. Wood
11. Leaves and greenery
12. Woven textiles—like linen or burlap
13. Glass

What's Our Entertaining and Partying Style?

Answer the following questions about how you typically celebrate and hang with friends to get ideas for the vibe of your wedding.

1. When we host friends at our home, they can usually expect:
   a. Competitive card games
   b. Some winetasting
   c. An impromptu dance party

2. We love getting invited to:
   a. Backyard BBQs
   b. Costume parties
   c. Black-tie soirees

3. Our favorite restaurant in town is:
   a. Our local pizza joint
   b. Whatever's new and just opened
   c. The tapas place where you can get a little of everything

4. The ideal Saturday for us is:
   a. Going on a hike or to the beach
   b. Hanging out at a fun bar
   c. Lounging at home

5. When something big happens in our lives, we celebrate by:
   a. Going out to a big dinner with our crew
   b. Honoring the moment with just the two of us
   c. Painting the town red

6. The ideal host/hostess gift is:
   a. A bottle of wine
   b. A gorgeous bouquet of flowers
   c. A game everyone can play together

7. When we host, we typically serve:
   a. A home-cooked meal
   b. Appetizers we picked up at the grocery store
   c. A selection of cookies and other goodies

8. Our primary role as a host/hostess is usually:
   a. Playing DJ
   b. Whipping up cocktails
   c. Making sure everyone is well-fed

9. During the week, we typically:
   a. Cook at home
   b. Go out to our favorite restaurants
   c. Make it a point to try new eateries in town

10. The best parties always have:
    a. Great food
    b. Awesome music
    c. Fun people

Must-Have Wedding Advice

Use this quiz as a place to jot down words of wisdom from a couple who's been there. Interview a pair of recently married friends to get their wedding-planning insight.

1. Favorite memory from your wedding:

   _____

   _____

2. Number one piece of advice for planning:

   _____

   _____

3. One thing every couple should do on their wedding day:

   _____

   _____

4. Thing you worried most about that didn't matter on the day of:

   _____

   _____

5. What you wish you spent more time planning:

   _____

   _____

6. What you wish you spent less time planning:

   _____

   _____

7. What you wish you spent more money on:

   _____

   _____

8. What you wish you spent less money on:

_____

_____

9. Décor item you could have lived without:

_____

_____

10. Vendor you think is most important to vet before hiring:

_____

_____

11. Logistics you wish you'd thought about:

_____

_____

What Wedding Activities Would We Like to Include?

It's fun to give guests something to do at your wedding besides eat and drink. Here are a plethora of options to consider.

- ☑ Dancing
- ☐ Karaoke
- ☑ Lawn games
- ☑ Lounge area for chilling
- ☑ Board or card games
- ☐ Wine, beer, or whiskey tasting
- ☑ Photo booth
- ☑ Slideshow or movie for guests to watch
- ☐ Artsy project, like a scrapbook guest book
- ☐ One big interactive game, like *Family Feud*
- ☑ Mad Libs or trivia at each table
- ☐ Guessing or voting, like for best cake flavor or where we're honeymooning

How Techie Do We Want Our Wedding to Be?

Some couples want their weddings to be completely high-tech; others want guests to keep their smartphones in their pockets. Do you want any of these aspects to be digital?

1. Create a wedding website -OR- relay necessary info in our invitations?
2. E-mail/Paperless Post save the dates -OR- paper stationery?
3. Tech-free ceremony -OR- people taking photos on their smartphones during?
4. Wear a GoPro during our wedding -OR- hire a videographer?
5. Use a wedding drone to capture our big day -OR- have a person on the ground?
6. Stream our wedding live to those who can't make it -OR- just send them photos/video after?
7. Officiant using iPad during ceremony -OR- a notebook/binder?
8. Digital guest book -OR- pen and paper?
9. Say vows we've written on our smartphones -OR- notecards?
10. Digital photo booth -OR- a simple backdrop for fun photos?
11. Cool lighting projected onto our cake -OR- icing décor? NEITHER
12. 3D printed cake topper -OR- something more traditional, like flowers?

What Role Should Social Media Play at Our Wedding?

These days, social media is an almost unavoidable part of your day. Decide how you want to incorporate it so you can make it work for you!

1. Do we prefer guests to refrain from posting on social media or are we cool with photos of our big day ending up online?

   _____

   _____

2. How should we communicate our social media wants to our guests?

   _____

   _____

3. Should we create a wedding hashtag for Instagram and other social platforms for guests to use?

   _____

   _____

4. What are some creative hashtag ideas we could consider?

   _____

   _____

5. How should we display or tell guests about our hashtag? (With a sign? Monogrammed cocktail napkins?)

   _____

   _____

6. How do we feel about live-Tweeting or Snapchatting our wedding? (Either us doing so or someone else?)

   _____

   _____

7. Are there certain parts of our big day during which we don't want social media to pay a role? (Like, no posting photos of us getting ready or of the ceremony?)

_____

_____

8. Would we consider using social media to crowdsource any parts of our wedding planning? (Like, which cake flavors to offer at the dessert station or which songs should play at the reception?)

_____

_____

9. What are some clever ways we've seen people use social media at past weddings or events we've attended? (Do any of them speak to us and our celebration?)

_____

_____

10. Do we have any funny social media moments—like old Facebook wall posts or messages from early in our relationship—that we want to display or reference at our wedding?

_____

_____

Must-Haves for Our Wedding Website

A wedding website can be an ecofriendly and easy way to share information with guests near and far. Use this quiz to help you determine the content of your wedding site by checking off all the things you want to include.

- ❑ The crucial details for the wedding and all wedding events—place, day, and time
- ❑ Information about transportation, hotels, and other logistics
- ❑ Photos of us
- ❑ Blurbs about everyone in our wedding party
- ❑ The story of how we met
- ❑ The story of how we got engaged
- ❑ Our registry information
- ❑ A place where guests can RSVP
- ❑ A message board where guests can connect before the wedding
- ❑ An interactive quiz asking guests their input on wedding details, like cake flavors and songs they want to hear at the reception
- ❑ Our favorite things to do in our wedding city for those traveling in for the weekend

2

Timing and Location

What Time of Year Is Ideal for Our Wedding?

If you don't already know exactly when you want to get married, savor the many options open to you!

1. Personal considerations: Are there certain seasons, months, or even dates that we prefer for one reason or another?

   _____

   _____

2. Guest considerations: Are there certain holidays or times of year when it may be more difficult for our loved ones to travel?

   _____

   _____

3. Vibe considerations: What time of year matches the type of wedding we want?

   _____

   _____

4. Anniversary considerations: When do we want to celebrate our marriage for years to come?

   _____

   _____

5. Temperature considerations: Are we looking for a snowy, winter wedding? Or a sunnier soiree?

   _____

   _____

6. Weather considerations: Do we mind having a chance of rain? Would a heat wave be a disaster?

_____

_____

7. Health considerations: Do either of us have allergies that come out during a particular time of the year?

_____

_____

8. Life considerations: Do we have any other important events on the horizon, like graduations, a baby on the way, birthdays, vacations, or other weddings?

_____

_____

9. Budget considerations: Would we prefer to get married in an off-season to help cut wedding costs?

_____

_____

10. Seasonal considerations: Are there certain flowers or foods we must have at our wedding?

_____

_____

What Day of the Week Is Best for Our Wedding?

Weddings do not have to be Saturday affairs. Ask yourself these questions to see which day is truly best for your event.

1. Personal considerations: Do we have an ideal day or date already in mind?

   _____

   _____

2. Timing considerations: Would we prefer a daytime or an evening wedding?

   _____

   _____

3. Budget considerations: Weekday weddings are typically less pricey—would we be willing to forgo a weekend wedding to save money?

   _____

   _____

4. Work considerations: Are we planning to take time off the week of our wedding? Would we be willing to if we choose to have a weekday wedding?

   _____

   _____

5. Guest considerations: Will many of our guests need to travel to attend our wedding? (If so, a weekend is usually best.)

   _____

   _____

6. Size considerations: Are we already considering a smaller wedding? (If so, a weekday could be a good option.)

_____

_____

7. Traffic considerations: Does our wedding city typically have a crazy rush hour? (Something to think about if you want to host a weekday wedding after work hours.)

_____

_____

8. Venue considerations: Do we have our hearts set on a certain place that's already booked for the weekend? Does the venue we want to choose allow weekday weddings?

_____

_____

9. Vibe considerations: Are we desiring a dance party? (A weekend wedding may be more ideal for guests to let loose.)

_____

_____

10. Formality considerations: Are we planning more of a low-key, backyard BBQ? Or do we want a more dressed-up, black-tie affair?

_____

_____

What Time of Day Do We Prefer for Our Wedding?

The time of your wedding should take into account several factors: where you're having your wedding, the guest list, your preferences, and more.

1. Personal considerations: Are we morning people or night owls?

   _____

   _____

2. Timing considerations: Is there a certain time of day we need to hold our ceremony, for religious or other reasons?

   _____

   _____

3. Logistical considerations: Would we like to have time for pictures in between our ceremony and reception? (If so, a morning or afternoon ceremony may be best.)

   _____

   _____

4. Vibe considerations: Do we want our celebration to be more laid-back or more of a party?

   _____

   _____

5. Attire considerations: Do we want our wedding to be more casual or more formal?

   _____

   _____

6. Food considerations: What kind of meal do we ideally want to serve?

_____

_____

7. Décor considerations: Do we picture twinkle lights or lanterns at our wedding? Or do we want lots of natural light?

_____

_____

8. Guest considerations: Are many guests traveling by car and need to return home the night of our wedding?

_____

_____

9. Lodging considerations: Would we like to avoid guests having to get hotel rooms and spend the night?

_____

_____

10. Honeymoon considerations: Are we planning to leave for our trip the night of our wedding?

_____

_____

Is a Destination Wedding Right for Us?

Destination weddings are always exciting. Is going abroad for your big day the right option for you two?

1. We love to travel.   **TRUE** ❏ | **FALSE** ❏

2. We prefer fewer wedding-related logistics.   **TRUE** ❏ | **FALSE** ❏

3. We get nervous or anxious about flying.   **TRUE** ❏ | **FALSE** ❏

4. We're totally cool planning from afar.   **TRUE** ❏ | **FALSE** ❏

5. We need to be able to meet vendors in person before the big day.   **TRUE** ❏ | **FALSE** ❏

6. We love the idea of an all-inclusive wedding that just allows us to show up.   **TRUE** ❏ | **FALSE** ❏

7. Most of our guests will be able and willing to travel.   **TRUE** ❏ | **FALSE** ❏

8. We have a special country or city that's meaningful to our relationship and us.   **TRUE** ❏ | **FALSE** ❏

9. We're okay with some guests declining due to high costs of travel.   **TRUE** ❏ | **FALSE** ❏

10. Many of our family members and friends live abroad.   **TRUE** ❏ | **FALSE** ❏

11. Packing a suitcase for our wedding week/weekend is no big deal.   **TRUE** ❏ | **FALSE** ❏

12. We're okay with potentially never seeing our venue before we book it.   **TRUE** ❏ | **FALSE** ❏

13. The location of our wedding is more important than anything else.   **TRUE** ❏ | **FALSE** ❏

What Destinations Appeal to Us Most?

If you're considering a destination wedding, the world is your oyster! Use these questions to narrow down your options.

1. A place we can drive to -OR- a place we'd need to fly to?
2. National -OR- international destination?
3. Beach -OR- city?
4. Forest -OR- countryside?
5. Place we've vacationed before -OR- totally new locale?
6. Familiar language and culture -OR- totally different?
7. Tropical, warm weather -OR- cozy, snowy weather?
8. A place where our family is from -OR- no family connection?
9. A place we can honeymoon after -OR- just a wedding location?
10. Total travel time under three hours -OR- over three hours?

3

Budgeting

All about the Budget:
Funding Our Wedding

Budgeting is maybe the least fun part of planning a wedding, but it's a necessary evil. Thinking ahead will help make funding your wedding way less stressful.

1. What budget do we feel comfortable with for our big day?

_____

_____

2. Who's paying and how much can they contribute?

_____

_____

3. How much can we contribute?

_____

_____

4. What are three things we want to splurge on or are worth spending a little more on?

_____

_____

5. What three things do we care less about and can skip entirely?

_____

_____

6. What three things should we try to save money on?

_____

_____

7. How do we plan to balance our wedding wants with the wants of those who are funding our wedding?

_____

_____

8. How involved in the planning do we want those who are funding it to be?

_____

_____

9. How are we going to ensure we don't go over budget?

_____

_____

10. How much should we put into a contingency or just-in-case fund?

_____

_____

What Did We Forget in Our Budget?

As you create your budget, be sure you don't skip these important items that can affect your bottom line. (Check with your vendors before signing contracts to see which fees apply to you!)

❑ Service fees and taxes

❑ Cake-cutting fee

❑ Tips

❑ Insurance

❑ Alterations

❑ Makeup/hair trials

❑ Postage for invitations

❑ Shipping costs

❑ Set-up/breakdown charges

❑ Corkage fee

❑ Audio/visual rentals (for microphones/speakers)

❑ Marriage license

❑ Overtime charges

How We'll Keep Our Budget in Check

Despite their best efforts, most couples go over budget in one area or another. Here are some strategies to think about ahead of time to minimize issues later.

1. How much we personally want to spend (if others are paying):

    _____

    _____

2. How we will keep track of our wedding spending:

    _____

    _____

3. Plan of action for when we want to go over budget on a given item:

    _____

    _____

4. How much over budget we can go on any one item:

    _____

    _____

5. How many options we will research for any one item or vendor before choosing:

    _____

    _____

6. How we'll decide what to cut from our wedding/wedding budget, if needed:

    _____

    _____

7. How we plan to deal with unexpected costs:

_____

_____

8. How we will deal with parents wanting to add more guests:

_____

_____

9. How we will keep track of what we've each compromised to fit our budget:

_____

_____

What Optional Wedding Details Can We Cut from Our Budget?

Here are some niceties that you might be able to do without to save money. Which ones can you eliminate?

- ❏ Paper RSVP cards
- ❏ Printed ceremony programs
- ❏ Favors
- ❏ Custom cocktails/signature drink
- ❏ Menus
- ❏ Place cards
- ❏ Custom signage
- ❏ Guest book
- ❏ Welcome bags
- ❏ Late-night snacks
- ❏ Transportation

How DIY Should We Get?

It's tempting to think you can handle a lot of wedding décor yourself. Before you jump in with both feet, however, ask yourselves these questions and answer honestly.

1. How crafty do we consider ourselves?

   _____

   _____

2. What kinds of crafts and projects do we enjoy doing?

   _____

   _____

3. What artistic talents do we have?

   _____

   _____

4. How much time do we have to dedicate to DIY projects?

   _____

   _____

5. How many DIY projects do we feel comfortable taking on?

   _____

   _____

6. Who might be able to help us with our wedding projects?

   _____

   _____

7. What aspects of our wedding do we think should be DIY?

   _____

   _____

8. What aspects of our wedding do we feel more comfortable renting or buying already done?

_____

_____

9. How do we feel about bringing the DIY items we make to our wedding— and potentially setting them up?

_____

_____

10. How do we feel about taking down those DIY items and packing them up postwedding?

_____

_____

Where Do We Register and What Do We Need?

Wedding registries can be a win-win for couples and their guests—you can offer your loved ones a range of gift options that you know you want . . . and guests can easily choose something within their budget that they are sure you'll be happy with.

1. What do we want?
   a. Cash
   b. Household items
   c. We'd prefer no gifts

2. Do we care what people get us?
   a. Yes, we'd rather register for things we can really use.
   b. Kind of—we don't really need much, but we don't want a bunch of random items either.
   c. No, people should just buy us whatever they want.

3. Where do we prefer to shop?
   a. Online
   b. In-store
   c. A combination of the two

4. What stores appeal to use most?
   a. Pottery Barn and Williams-Sonoma
   b. Amazon and Target
   c. Urban Outfitters and Anthropologie

5. If we got cash, what would we use it for?
   a. Honeymoon
   b. Savings
   c. Down payment for a house

6. What items in our home need upgrades?
   a. Appliances, like our toaster and blender
   b. Linens, like sheets and towels

   c. General décor, like pillows and artwork

7. How do we want to choose what we register for?
   a. See items in person and get help from someone at the store
   b. Create a wish list online ourselves, without going to stores
   c. Go look at items in the store, but create the registry online

8. Who should create the registry?
   a. Me
   b. You
   c. Both of us together

9. How many places do we want to register at?
   a. One
   b. Two
   c. Three

10. What price point do we feel comfortable with for gifts?
   a. We'll put a mix of stuff on there at varying prices
   b. Nothing over $200
   c. Nothing over $100

4

The Guest List and Invitations

What's the Ideal Size Wedding for Us?

Use the following questions to determine how to shape your guest list.

1. What's more important: Saying hello to everyone at our wedding or having longer conversations with a few people?

   _____

   _____

2. Do we like the idea of going table to table during dinner to greet guests or prefer that everyone is able to sit at one big table?

   _____

   _____

3. Are we more extroverted or introverted?

   _____

   _____

4. Are we drawn to large parties or prefer more intimate gatherings?

   _____

   _____

5. Does the idea of having a large crowd at our wedding excite us or intimidate us?

   _____

   _____

6. Does the idea of having a small crowd at our wedding make us happy or worried we'll miss having more people there/feel too exclusive?

   _____

   _____

7. Does our budget allow us to have the wedding we want while inviting everyone we want to have there?

_____

_____

8. Does our ideal venue have any restrictions or minimums regarding guests?

_____

_____

9. Do we have large families or circles of friends that we want to invite or are our lists generally on the smaller side?

_____

_____

10. Do our wedding priorities line up with having more guests or fewer?

_____

_____

Planning with Blended Families

These days, many couples come from divorced families and/or they may already have children of their own. Use this quiz to guide discussion about how to make your loved ones feel special on your big day and what logistics may be involved.

1. What things do we need to think about or consider when it comes to our families on our wedding day?

   _____

   _____

2. What concerns do we have when it comes to our families?

   _____

   _____

3. How will we manage different sets of parents contributing money and/or opinions about our wedding?

   _____

   _____

4. Do we need to think about any seating considerations for the ceremony and reception for our families?

   _____

   _____

5. How will we divvy up special tasks for parents (walking down the aisle, dances) if we have more than one father or mother figure?

   _____

   _____

6. What are some ways we can honor all of our parents and designate them? (Special boutonnieres or corsages? Names in the programs?)

_____

_____

7. Is there anyone we *don't* want to honor, and how will we deal with that?

_____

_____

8. Are there any people who aren't our parents but who have acted like parents to us that we would like to designate?

_____

_____

9. How would we like to include our child(ren) into our ceremony?

_____

_____

10. What special attire would we like our child(ren) to wear?

_____

_____

11. Are there any other ways we'd like to include our child(ren)? (Like a special dance or speech?)

_____

_____

Where Do We Want to Draw the Guest List Line?

Guest lists can balloon quickly if you're not careful. Use these questions to determine a cutoff.

1. First cousins?   **YES** ❏ **NO** ❏
2. Second cousins?   **YES** ❏ **NO** ❏
3. Extended family we only see at the reunion?   **YES** ❏ **NO** ❏
4. Family friends?   **YES** ❏ **NO** ❏
5. Parents' friends we've met?   **YES** ❏ **NO** ❏
6. Parents' friends we've never met?   **YES** ❏ **NO** ❏
7. Kids?   **YES** ❏ **NO** ❏
8. Kids who are not family?   **YES** ❏ **NO** ❏
9. Childhood friends we don't see or speak to regularly?   **YES** ❏ **NO** ❏
10. College friends we haven't seen in person since college?   **YES** ❏ **NO** ❏

Do We Need to Invite This Person?

Use the following questions to help you determine who makes the cut if there are certain potential guests about whom you're on the fence.

1. Has this person met your intended?   **YES** ❑ | **NO** ❑
2. Have we seen this person within the past two years? **YES** ❑ | **NO** ❑
3. Have we seen this person within the past six months? **YES** ❑ | **NO** ❑
4. Do we communicate with this person regularly?   **YES** ❑ | **NO** ❑
5. Is our main mode of communication social media?   **YES** ❑ | **NO** ❑
6. Did we get invited to his/her wedding (within the past year)? **YES** ❑ | **NO** ❑
7. When we picture our big day, is this person there? **YES** ❑ | **NO** ❑
8. Do we see ourselves spending time with this person in the future? **YES** ❑ | **NO** ❑
9. Would we make an effort to see this person more often? **YES** ❑ | **NO** ❑
10. Will we truly regret not including this person?   **YES** ❑ | **NO** ❑

What Are Your Invitation Must-Haves?

You'll find endless variations on invitation options. Answer these questions to help you focus your preferences.

1. Colorful -OR- white?
2. Patterned -OR- nondecorative?
3. Textured paper -OR- smooth?
4. Extra-thick paper -OR- card stock?
5. Letterpress -OR- printed or hand-drawn?
6. Gold foil -OR- no metallic elements?
7. Envelope liner -OR- traditional envelope?
8. Paper RSVP card -OR- digital/online?
9. Bolder font -OR- softer font?
10. Simple design -OR- super eye-catching?
11. Include photography -OR- keep it purely graphic?

Determining Your Ideal Invitation Wording

Breaking down your invitations into sections can help make choosing the wording less overwhelming.

1. For the host line:
   a. "Together with our/their families"
   b. Listing parents' names as hosts (if they're paying)
   c. No host line

2. For our names:
   a. Full names: first, middle, last
   b. Just first and last names
   c. Just first names

3. For the invitation line:
   a. Formal: "Request the honor of your presence at . . ."
   b. Formal: "Request the pleasure of your company at . . ."
   c. Less formal: Would love you to join us at . . ./Invite you to celebrate . . ."

4. For the event line:
   a. "The marriage of their children . . ." (if your parents are hosting)
   b. "Our marriage . . ." (if you're hosting)
   c. "A celebration of love . . ."

5. For the information line:
   a. Formal: Spell out day/time/location in full (i.e., "Saturday, the twelfth of July, four-thirty in the afternoon")
   b. Semiformal: Spell out day, put time in numbers (i.e., "Saturday, the twelfth of July, 4:30 P.M.")
   c. Casual: Keep it simple ("July 12, 4:30 P.M.")

6. For the description of the party:

   a. "Dinner and dancing to follow."
   b. "Joy and laughter to follow."
   c. "One amazing party to follow."

7. For the reply card:

   a. Traditional formal: "Accepts with pleasure/Declines with regret"
   b. Traditional semiformal: "Happily accepts/Regretfully declines"
   c. Nontraditional casual: "Can't wait to be there/Will be there in spirit"

8. For the envelope address:

   a. Spell out everything formally—full names, streets, apartment numbers
   b. Use full names but abbreviate words like "street" and "apartment," and use numbers
   c. Just names (without Mr., Ms., etc.) and abbreviate as much as possible

5

The Ceremony

What's Our Ceremony Style?

Circle five words in the following list that you could use to describe your ideal ceremony.

1. Personal
2. Religious
3. Traditional
4. Modern
5. Romantic
6. Straightforward
7. Short
8. Interactive
9. Unique
10. Elaborate
11. Inclusive
12. Cultural

What Ceremony Venue Will Suit Us Best?

Choosing your ceremony location is one of the biggest decisions you'll make. Use these considerations to help you make the choice that's best for you.

1. Vibe considerations: What general look and feel do we want for our wedding ceremony? Do we want an indoor or outdoor venue? Rustic or formal? Traditional or modern?

   _____

   _____

2. Personal considerations: Do we want to wed in a location that has personal meaning or significance to us or our families?

   _____

   _____

3. Décor considerations: How would we like our ceremony site to look? (Flowers? Backdrop? Altar? Chuppah?)

   _____

   _____

4. Officiant considerations: Would we prefer to use an officiant associated with a given venue or choose our own?

   _____

   _____

5. Religious considerations: Is having our ceremony in a house of worship a must?

   _____

   _____

6. Logistical considerations: Is it ideal for us to have guests travel from one location to another for the reception? Will we provide transportation?

_____

_____

7. Timing considerations: How long will guests need to wait between the ceremony ending and the reception starting?

_____

_____

8. Comfort considerations: What seating does the venue provide? Is the seating situated inside or outside? Shade or sun?

_____

_____

9. Photography considerations: How important is it to us that the venue is photogenic? (When you look at venues, be sure to ask if there are any restrictions for photography and/or videography.)

_____

_____

Our Ideal Officiant

Use the following quiz to check off the personality traits you'd want to see in the person who will perform the marriage ceremony.

- ❑ Someone we've known for a long time
- ❑ Someone who shares our cultural background
- ❑ Someone who shares our faith(s)
- ❑ Someone with a sense of humor
- ❑ Someone whose marriage we respect
- ❑ Someone who's serious
- ❑ Someone who was close with us when we first met or started dating
- ❑ Someone with a strong presence
- ❑ Someone with great speaking skills
- ❑ Someone creative who can give us ideas for the ceremony
- ❑ Someone we can trust to create a ceremony that reflects us

Ceremony Décor

Instagram, wedding blogs, and Pinterest can offer you thousands of ceremony décor options. This quiz distills some of the most popular choices for you to consider.

1. Chuppah/archway -OR- simple platform?
2. Paper flower or ribbon backdrop -OR- something natural, like a tree?
3. Aisle runner -OR- rose petals strewn down the walkway?
4. Twinkle lights -OR- candles?
5. Hanging glass lanterns -OR- paper lanterns?
6. Lots of colorful flowers -OR- all greenery?
7. Flower arrangements flanking us -OR- decorative pillars?
8. Chairs arranged traditionally -OR- in the round?
9. Guests seated on traditional chairs -OR- on furniture pieces, benches, or hay bales?
10. If indoors, fabric wall draping -OR- walls as they are?
11. Uplighting -OR- natural light?

What Ceremony Traditions Do We Want to Include?

You may already be considering certain traditions you want to incorporate into your big day. This quiz will make sure you don't forget any!

1. Not seeing each other before the ceremony   *THINK* *- Amy arranging* *- timing logistics* *for photos*
   a. Totally a must
   b. Totally indifferent
   c. Totally not happening

2. Seating our guests on two distinct sides
   a. Totally a must
   b. Totally indifferent
   c. Totally not happening

3. Father walking the bride down the aisle *+ Mom?!*
   a. Totally a must
   b. Totally indifferent
   c. Totally not happening

4. The bride covering her face with a blusher veil
   a. Totally a must
   b. Totally indifferent
   c. Totally not happening

5. The bride entering to a wedding march (Wagner's "Bridal Chorus")
   a. Totally a must
   b. Totally indifferent   *→ Clair de Lune*
   c. Totally not happening

6. Getting married by a member of the clergy, judge, or professional officiant
   a. Totally a must
   b. Totally indifferent *- Pastor Jen!*
   c. Totally not happening

7. Religious or cultural aspects like jumping the broom, lighting a unity candle, or breaking the glass
   a. Totally a must
   b. Totally indifferent
   c. Totally not happening

   up for ideas!

8. Traditional vows / *Modern*
   a. Totally a must
   b. Totally indifferent
   c. Totally not happening

9. Exchange of wedding bands
   a. Totally a must
   b. Totally indifferent
   c. Totally not happening

10. The handfasting ritual, during which the bride and groom's hands are tied with ribbon to signify their union
    a. Totally a must
    b. Totally indifferent
    c. Totally not happening

11. Bride having something old, new, borrowed, and blue ⇒ *Broncos garter!*
    a. Totally a must
    b. Totally indifferent
    c. Totally not happening

What Nontraditional Ceremony Elements Do We Want to Include?

Maybe you've seen some of these unusual components at other weddings, or you are open to unique ceremony styles. Take the quiz to find out.

1. Walking down the aisle together at the start of the ceremony
   a. Totally a must
   b. Totally indifferent
   c. Totally not happening

2. Not having an aisle at all
   a. Totally a must
   b. Totally indifferent
   c. Totally not happening

3. Having our guests stand around us in a circle
   a. Totally a must
   b. Totally indifferent
   c. Totally not happening

4. Getting married by a friend or family member
   a. Totally a must
   b. Totally indifferent
   c. Totally not happening

5. Creating a time capsule during the ceremony to open at our one-year anniversary
   a. Totally a must
   b. Totally indifferent
   c. Totally not happening

5? 10? 20?

reception?

6. Writing our own vows
   a. Totally a must
   b. Totally indifferent
   c. Totally not happening

7. Having friends or family members give readings or speeches during the ceremony
   a. Totally a must
   b. Totally indifferent
   c. Totally not happening

8. Asking our guests to pass our rings around—a ring-warming ceremony—to one another before we exchange them
   a. Totally a must
   b. Totally indifferent
   c. Totally not happening

   something different

9. Toasting each other with our favorite beverage during the ceremony
   a. Totally a must
   b. Totally indifferent
   c. Totally not happening

10. Having audience participation as part of the ceremony
   a. Totally a must
   b. Totally indifferent
   c. Totally not happening

   → call & response?

Deciding Whether or Not
to Do a First Look

Some couples love the idea of a "first look," when you see each other pre-ceremony. Others aren't as into it and prefer to have the big reveal at the ceremony itself. This quiz will help you decide which way you're leaning.

1. We plan to wake up together the morning of the wedding.   **TRUE** ❏ | **FALSE** ☑

2. We like the idea of seeing each other before the ceremony.   **TRUE** ❏ / **FALSE** ❏

3. We want to take photos together before the ceremony.   **TRUE** ❏ / **FALSE** ❏

4. We are superstitious.   **TRUE** ❏ | **FALSE** ☑

5. We'd prefer to have more time to get ready or sleep in.   **TRUE** ❏ | **FALSE** ☑

6. We'd rather read notes we've written to each other before the wedding than see each other.   **TRUE** ☑ | **FALSE** ❏

7. We'd prefer to have our photographer start shooting later rather than earlier.   **TRUE** ❏ | **FALSE** ☑

8. We don't want/need to do an official first look.   **TRUE** ❏ / **FALSE** ❏

9. We want to get ready together so there's no need for a first look.   **TRUE** ❏ | **FALSE** ☑

10. We want to do a first look, but we want it to be private and less formal—no photographer.   **TRUE** ❏ / **FALSE** ❏

Ideas for Your Recessional

Use this list to discover what you want to happen when your ceremony ends to celebrate your marriage. Circle as many that appeal to you, then narrow your ideas down.

1. Guests throwing rose petals
2. Guests tossing confetti
3. Guests tossing birdseed
4. Butterfly or bird release
5. Upbeat song playing
6. Love song playing
7. Marching band or spirited live music
8. Guests singing a song
9. Doing a coordinated dance down the aisle
10. Walking hand in hand to classical music
11. Something dramatic, like a fun light show

6

The Reception

Creating the Ideal Cocktail Hour

Cocktail hour isn't just a time for drinks—or for you to take photos: In fact, it's the beginning of the celebratory festivities. Use this quiz to brainstorm ideas on how to make it your own.

1. The location: Where do we picture having cocktail hour? Indoors, outdoors, in a particular location within a venue?

   _____

   _____

2. The bar: Would we like to offer a signature cocktail? What are some of our initial ideas? (His and hers? Something we drank on vacation?)

   _____

   _____

3. The food: Fancy, comfort, or classic?

   _____

   _____

4. The food volume and variety: Do we want to provide our guests with a snack or do they need to be tied over for a later meal?

   _____

   _____

5. The food service: Passed appetizers or stations?

   _____

   _____

6. The entertainment: Fun playlist or live music?

   _____

   _____

7. The activities: Lawn games, word games (like Mad Libs), board games, or no activities needed?

_____

_____

8. The length: Quickie forty-five-minute cocktail session or a full hour?

_____

_____

9. The logistics: Would we like to join our guests for cocktail hour or take photos during this time?

_____

_____

10. The guests' comfort: Can we offer comfy places to sit for older folks? What are some fun ideas for nonalcoholic options for those who don't imbibe?

_____

_____

What Words Best Describe Our Ideal Reception?

Circle five words to describe your ideal reception.

1. Action-packed
2. Distinctive
3. Intimate
4. Fun
5. Musical
6. Cozy
7. Relaxed
8. Something for everyone
9. Memorable
10. Elegant
11. Organized
12. Open-ended

What Reception Venue Will Suit Us Best?

Besides your ceremony location, choosing a reception venue is perhaps the biggest decision you'll make. Use this quiz to be sure you take all possible considerations into account.

1. Vibe considerations: What general look and feel do we want for our reception? Do we want a place that's indoors or outdoors? Formal or more casual?

   _____

   _____

2. Personal considerations: Would we prefer to host guests at a family home or a place that's meaningful to us?

   _____

   _____

3. Décor considerations: What do we picture our reception to look like?

   _____

   _____

4. Musical considerations: Is it crucial that the reception venue can host a band?

   _____

   _____

5. Logistical considerations: Should the reception be the same place as the ceremony? How will the venue be transformed after we say our vows?

   _____

   _____

6. Timing considerations: How late do we want our reception to go?

_____

_____

7. Comfort considerations: Do we have older guests, kids, or those with special needs? (You'll want to factor in accessibility, how loud the room gets, bathrooms, etc.)

_____

_____

8. Rental considerations: Do we prefer the reception venue to provide tables, chairs, tabletop necessities, etc.?

_____

_____

9. Photography considerations: Do we want to take photos at our reception? Ideally, what are our expectations for these images?

_____

_____

10. Guest considerations: Would we like guests to be able to stay on-site at our reception venue?

_____

_____

What Reception Traditions Do We Want to Include?

Do you want all the traditional parts of a reception? Ask yourselves these questions.

1. The receiving line
   a. Totally a must
   b. Totally indifferent
   c. Totally not happening

2. The grand entrance
   a. Totally a must
   b. Totally indifferent
   c. Totally not happening

3. The first dance
   a. Totally a must
   b. Totally indifferent
   c. Totally not happening

4. The father-of-the-bride speech
   a. Totally a must
   b. Totally indifferent
   c. Totally not happening

5. The best-man speech
   a. Totally a must
   b. Totally indifferent
   c. Totally not happening

6. The father/daughter and mother/son dances
   a. Totally a must
   b. Totally indifferent
   c. Totally not happening

7. The bouquet and garter toss
   a. Totally a must
   b. Totally indifferent
   c. Totally not happening

8. The cutting of the cake
   a. Totally a must
   b. Totally indifferent
   c. Totally not happening

9. Any traditional, cultural, or religious dances and ceremonies (like the hora)
   a. Totally a must
   b. Totally indifferent
   c. Totally not happening

10. The grand sendoff
    a. Totally a must
    b. Totally indifferent
    c. Totally not happening

What Logistical Considerations Should We Be Aware of When Choosing a Ceremony and/or Reception Venue?

Here are some factors you might not have considered that can have a big impact on your overall celebration.

1. Are we okay with having a venue curfew? (Some require the music to shut off at a certain time due to noise restrictions.)

   _____

   _____

2. Do any of our guests have a hard time getting around/might need assistance walking over sand or gravel and lots of stairs?

   _____

   _____

3. How wheelchair-friendly do we need our venue(s) to be?

   _____

   _____

4. Would we be willing to rent a generator if needed? (Typical with barn weddings!)

   _____

   _____

5. Does the venue need to have its own bathrooms or would we be okay with renting them?

   _____

   _____

6. Is it important to us to be able to bring in our own alcohol?

_____

_____

7. Does the venue need to be kid-friendly and/or kid-safe?

_____

_____

8. Does the bride/brides or our guests plan to wear high heels? (Grass can be tricky with heels!)

_____

_____

9. Do we want the aisle to be a smooth path or are we okay with cobblestone or sand?

_____

_____

10. Do we prefer to choose a venue that comes with tables, linens, and so on or would we like to rent those items separately?

_____

_____

Reception Styling

Once you've chosen a location, you might be able to make further choices that can really affect what the reception will look like.

1. Round tables -OR- long tables?
2. Tablecloths -OR- raw wood tables?
3. Pattered linens -OR- solid color?
4. Fabric draping around the venue -OR- bare walls?
5. Twinkle lights -OR- uplighting?
6. Sweetheart table -OR- sit with our guests?
7. Checkered dance floor -OR- wood?
8. Tea light candles -OR- candelabras?
9. White folding chairs -OR- wood vineyard chairs?
10. White china -OR- colored/patterned?
11. Clear glassware -OR- colored?

7

Décor and Food

Our Favorite Flowers

Use the following list of popular wedding flowers to guide the types of blooms you want for your celebration. Circle as many that appeal to you. (And don't worry if you have to do an online image search to know what they are—that's perfectly normal!)

1. Roses
2. Peonies
3. Tulips
4. Calla lilies
5. Lilies of the valley
6. Hydrangeas
7. Gardenias
8. Sweet peas
9. Baby's breath
10. Orchids
11. Daisies
12. Dahlias
13. Carnations

Finding Our Floral Style

Are you "married" to a certain style of flowers? Take this quiz to decide.

1. Our floral philosophy is:
   a. The more, the merrier
   b. Picked flowers soon wilt
   c. Flowers are pretty but not essential

2. For the bride: What type of bouquet appeals to you the most?
   a. Wild, natural-style
   b. Tightly packed with flowers
   c. Oversized and cascading

3. For the groom: What would you ideally want your boutonniere to include?
   a. Herbs and greens
   b. Feathers
   c. A bright bloom

4. When we picture our ceremony, the flowers are:
   a. In an archway above us
   b. Positioned on either side of where we're standing
   c. Just in the bride's hand as a bouquet

5. When we picture our reception tables, the flowers are:
   a. Garlands going down the center of each
   b. Large flower arrangements
   c. Grouped collections of bud vases

6. What types of flowers do we like most?
   a. Ruffled, layered blooms (like garden roses and ranunculus)
   b. Tiny blooms (chamomile and lily of the valley)
   c. Large petals or interestingly shaped blooms (tulips, irises, and protea)

7. If budget was not a factor, which of the following would we love to see at our wedding?
   a. Flower garlands draped across the ceiling
   b. Walls of greenery used as backdrops around the space
   c. Large trees brought in to decorate the room

8. Which type of small plant appeals to us most?

    a. Succulents
    b. Air plants
    c. Cacti

9. What greenery appeals to us most?

    a. Ferns
    b. Eucalyptus
    c. Myrtle

10. What would be our worst floral nightmare?

    a. Not getting the exact flowers we want on our big day
    b. Overspending on flowers
    c. Not having enough flowers

What Do We Want Our Flowers In?

Use this list to get ideas for displaying your flowers, if you're doing traditional arrangements.

- ❑ Wooden crates or boxes
- ❑ Standard glass vases
- ❑ Milk glass vases
- ❑ Mercury glass vases
- ❑ Silver teapots
- ❑ Rustic metal containers
- ❑ Tall topiary containers
- ❑ Containers filled with rocks, pearls, or gems
- ❑ Mason jars
- ❑ Vintage coffee and tea tins
- ❑ Glass bottles
- ❑ Clay pots

Narrowing Down Our Floral Wants

If you know you want flowers, this quiz can help you focus your decisions to maximize your floral budget.

1. In-season flowers -OR- specific flowers we know we want?
2. Flowers as our décor focal point -OR- just part of the overall look?
3. Colorful blooms -OR- neutrals?
4. Mostly greenery -OR- mostly flowers -OR- half and half?
5. Loose, whimsical flowers -OR- tighter, formal arrangements?
6. More flowers for the ceremony -OR- more flowers at the reception?
7. Flowers on every table -OR- a mix of flowers and props?
8. Bridesmaids' bouquets that are mini versions of the bride's -OR- bouquets that coordinate but don't match?
9. Color of flowers more important -OR- types of flowers?
10. Letting our florist guide our floral decisions -OR- us leading the way?

Additional Décor Ideas

Use this list to help you think of other pretty details that can coordinate with your flowers and your tabletop items. Check off any you might like.

- ❑ Vintage books
- ❑ Lanterns
- ❑ Terrariums
- ❑ Paper flowers
- ❑ Herbs at each place setting
- ❑ Printed menus
- ❑ Ribbon or tassel banners
- ❑ Marquee letters
- ❑ Rustic signs
- ❑ Framed photos
- ❑ Fresh fruit

Choosing Table Names

Use this list to come up with ideas for designating your tables so guests can find their seats and you can add some personality to your big day. Jot down your own ideas, too!

- ❑ Standard table numbers
- ❑ Cities we've traveled to
- ❑ Places we've lived together
- ❑ Favorite TV shows or movies
- ❑ Favorite literary figures
- ❑ Superheroes
- ❑ Special landmarks to our relationship
- ❑ Words for "love" in other languages
- ❑ Names that highlight an outdoor hobby of ours, like national parks or constellations
- ❑ Colors
- ❑ Favorite bands
- ❑ Famous couples
- ❑ Animals
- ❑ Significant years in our lives

Gifts for Your Guests

While sending your guests home with something special isn't required, the idea may appeal to you. Use this quiz to discover the best favor option for your big day and jot down specific ideas as you go.

1. Forgoing favors: Always an option if your budget is tight.

   _____

   _____

2. Something edible: Monogrammed cookies, mini-champagne bottles with custom labels or other festive treats.

   _____

   _____

3. Something that reflects your wedding city or state: Leis if you're getting hitched in Hawaii, for instance.

   _____

   _____

4. Something personal to you two: A favor that reflects your favorite hobby, movie, or other core characteristic.

   _____

   _____

5. Something charitable: Let guests know that you've made a donation to a cause you care about.

   _____

   _____

6. Something that's part of the décor: Tell guests to take flowers from the table or items you've used to decorate the venue.

   _____

   _____

7. Something for the day after: Send guests home with "hangover" kits.

_____

_____

8. Something practical: Offer bottled water and healthy snacks at the end of the night.

_____

_____

9. Something experiential: Host an afterparty instead of handing out favors.

_____

_____

10. Something celebratory: Give guests sparklers or confetti packets to light or toss at the end of the event.

_____

_____

Our Dining and Eating Personalities

Your wedding-day meal can reflect your everyday food preferences. Use this quiz to shape your reception dining experience.

1. Favorite meal of the day:
   a. Breakfast/brunch
   b. Lunch
   c. Dinner

2. When we go out to eat, we always sit:
   a. Inside
   b. Outside

3. Our ideal restaurant table is:
   a. In a cozy nook
   b. At the community table where we can chat with other people
   c. At the bar

4. We always order _____ in addition to our meal:
   a. An appetizer
   b. A salad
   c. A dessert

5. Our ideal meal style is:
   a. Shared plates
   b. Individual entrées
   c. Buffet

6. When it comes to food prep, we prefer:
   a. Not seeing the kitchen or food staff—we like the illusion
   b. Being able to see into the kitchen
   c. Cooking our own food, like at a fondue or Korean BBQ place

7. Our favorite cuisine type:
   a. Hearty and filling, like Italian or Mexican
   b. Fresh and light, like fish and lots of greens
   c. Meaty and traditional, like steak and potatoes

8. Our ideal ordering style is:
    a. Each getting one big entrée
    b. Sharing tapas or small plates
    c. Choosing two starters and splitting a main

9. Our ideal mealtime is:
    a. In the morning, but not too early
    b. Late afternoon
    c. Nighttime

10. Food is best when:
    a. Shared
    b. Enjoyed slowly
    c. Perfectly prepared

Discovering Our Wedding Meal Priorities

The main meal your guests eat leaves an impression on the party itself. But what should you serve? Get a handle on your options with this quiz.

1. We consider ourselves foodies. **TRUE** ❑ | **FALSE** ❑

2. We tend to be picky eaters. **TRUE** ❑ | **FALSE** ❑

3. We want our food to be the focus of our reception. **TRUE** ❑ | **FALSE** ❑

4. The type of food at our wedding is less important than the food tasting good and having enough of it. **TRUE** ❑ | **FALSE** ❑

5. Incorporating family or cultural dishes is important to us. **TRUE** ❑ | **FALSE** ❑

6. Having a wide variety of foods to accommodate different tastes and palettes is important to us. **TRUE** ❑ | **FALSE** ❑

7. Giving guests a choice of two or three items will suffice. **TRUE** ❑ | **FALSE** ❑

8. We have, or many of our guests have, dietary restrictions we want to consider. **TRUE** ❑ | **FALSE** ❑

9. We'd like our menu to reflect special meals or foods that have significance to our relationship. **TRUE** ❑ | **FALSE** ❑

10. Having in-season foods and ingredients is a priority to us. **TRUE** ❑ | **FALSE** ❑

All about the Bar

Some people think the bar is a significant part of the reception; others don't want it to be a focus of the day. These questions will help you figure out what's right for your event.

1. When it comes to drinking, we are:
   a. Total partiers and proud of it
   b. Likely to imbibe every now and then
   c. Not super into alcohol

2. Our ideal wedding bar includes:
   a. Craft beer
   b. A fun signature drink
   c. A little bit of everything

3. At our wedding, it's most important to offer:
   a. Welcome drinks
   b. Nightcaps

4. When it comes to beverage tastings, we prefer:
   a. Whiskey
   b. Coffee
   c. Wine

5. How important is having a champagne toast?
   a. It's a tradition—we want to have one.
   b. No one we know drinks bubbly; let's skip it.
   c. We'd rather just offer champagne at the bar.

6. What nonalcoholic drink station appeals to us most?
   a. Lemonade bar, with fruit and herbs
   b. Coffee bar, with sugar options and chocolate
   c. Hot chocolate bar, with marshmallows and other toppings

7. If we do a signature drinks, we'd prefer to have:
   a. His and hers offerings—our go-tos when we go out
   b. Cocktails that mean something to our relationship
   c. Drinks that fit the venue setting/location

8. When it comes to cocktails, we're into:
   a. Classics, like the Old Fashioned and Moscow Mule
   b. Modern drinks, like the Cosmopolitan and Long Island Ice Tea
   c. Beer and wine drinks, like the Black and Tan and Mimosa

9. When it comes to wine:
   a. We want to choose specific bottles—we're winos for sure.
   b. We want to offer the basics—a red and a white.
   c. We want to pick wines from a place we've visited—that will make the bar more personal.

10. When it comes to beer:
    a. We're fine with a cheap keg.
    b. We like small-batch breweries.
    c. We're not into beer, but we want to have some for guests.

Our Sweet-Tooth Styles

From personalized candy bars to elaborate three-tier cakes, reception desserts can be simple or ornate. Use your everyday preferences to help build your wedding-day sweet offerings.

1. Favorite cake flavor:
   a. Yours: _____
   b. Mine: _____

2. Favorite type of pie:
   a. Yours: _____
   b. Mine: _____

3. Favorite fancy dessert:
   a. Yours: _____
   b. Mine: _____

4. Favorite classic or traditional dessert:
   a. Yours: _____
   b. Mine: _____

5. Favorite ice cream flavor:
   a. Yours: _____
   b. Mine: _____

6. Favorite ice cream topping:
   a. Yours: _____
   b. Mine: _____

7. Favorite dessert from a restaurant:
   a. Yours: _____
   b. Mine: _____

8. Favorite international dessert or something we've tried on vacation:
   a. Yours: _____
   b. Mine: _____

9. Favorite drink to go with dessert:
   a. Yours: _____
   b. Mine: _____

10. Favorite way to enjoy dessert (buffet style, have our own plates, share with each other):
   a. Yours: _____
   b. Mine: _____

Wedding Dessert Brainstorm

Do you envision an elaborate wedding dessert or something simple? Ask yourselves what suits you most.

1. Traditional wedding cake -OR- pie?
2. Individual desserts for each guest -OR- a few big ones for everyone to share?
3. Fancy desserts (like crème brûlée) -OR- homey treats (like cookies and brownies)?
4. Variety of sweets -OR- a couple of options?
5. Plated dessert -OR- dessert bar/buffet?
6. Chocolate and vanilla -OR- fruit-focused sweets?
7. Ice cream sundae bar -OR- s'mores station?
8. Candy -OR- popcorn buffet?
9. Coffee -OR- tea with dessert?
10. Port -OR- whiskey with dessert?

8

Style

For the Bride: Your Personal Style

Many people want their wedding-day style to match who they are on a daily basis. (But your wedding could also be a fun opportunity to mix things up, too!) Ask yourself these questions to help you get a sense of your overall style.

1. If you could sum up your everyday style in three words, what would they be?

    _____

    _____

2. Who are your personal style icons? (Could be people whose style you admire or people whose style you like to emulate.)

    _____

    _____

3. Are you more apt to wear a dress and heels or a T-shirt and jeans?

    _____

    _____

4. What's your favorite or go-to outfit and why do you love it?

    _____

    _____

5. What's your absolute favorite dress that you've ever worn or owned? What about it made it amazing? (The fit, the color, the style?)

    _____

    _____

6. Do you enjoy getting dressed up or look at it as a hassle?

    _____

    _____

7. Do you want your overall look for your wedding to be similar to your everyday style or would you prefer to do something different or unexpected?

_____

_____

8. Is there anything you feel strongly about wearing, or not wearing, on your wedding day? (Like a veil, a certain color shoes, etc.)

_____

_____

9. What are your wedding wear priorities? (Comfort, an amazing overall look, keeping things traditional?)

_____

_____

10. When you picture your walk down the aisle, do you imagine a fairy-tale look, a garden party vibe, or a high-fashion ambiance?

_____

_____

For the Bride: What Should I Wear?

Here are some common bridal styles. Use this list to help stylists at bridal stores show you options that match your preferences.

1. White -OR- cream gown?
2. Traditional -OR- color?
3. Long gown -OR- short?
4. Tulle skirt -OR- taffeta?
5. Ball gown -OR- formfitting?
6. Beading -OR- sequins?
7. Lace -OR- satin?
8. Strapless -OR- straps?
9. Sleeves -OR- sleeveless?
10. Gorgeous from the front -OR- amazing back?
11. Low cut -OR- more modest?
12. One gown for the whole night -OR- change into another?
13. Asymmetrical -OR- symmetrical design?
14. Sheer, floating layers -OR- thicker material?
15. Velvet -OR- silk detailing?
16. Tiny buttons up the back -OR- concealed zipper?

For the Bride: What Accessories Should I Wear?

Bridal accessories can take your whole look up a notch. Think about these options.

1. Veil -OR- no veil?
2. Long veil -OR- medium-length -OR- birdcage?
3. Headpiece -OR- flowers in your hair?
4. Statement necklace -OR- pretty belt?
5. White shoes -OR- metallic -OR- a color?
6. Formal hairstyle -OR- loose curls?
7. Just your rings -OR- other bling?
8. Heirloom jewelry -OR- something new?
9. Carry a purse -OR- give my essentials to my maid of honor?
10. Wrap -OR- jacket in case it's cold?

For the Bride: What's My Ideal Dress-Shopping Experience?

There are almost as many ways to shop as there are dresses out there! Answer these questions to be sure your shopping trips are fun and positive, not stressful and uncomfortable.

1. How do you want to shop?
   a. In bridal salons
   b. At sample sales
   c. Online

2. How many stores/websites/sales do you want to visit?
   a. At least ten
   b. Five should be more than enough
   c. Two or three, or one if I can find a dress on the first trip

3. Who do you want in your shopping entourage?
   a. Just my mom/parent and a close friend
   b. My bridal party
   c. As many close friends and female family members who want to come

4. What type of stores/websites/sales do you want to shop at?
   a. High-end bridal stores that carry top designers
   b. Places that feature little-known designers and dressmakers
   c. Chain retailers, like David's Bridal or Nordstrom

5. How much research do you want to do beforehand?
   a. I want to have a firm grasp of which designers I like and the cuts/styles I prefer.
   b. I will make a Pinterest board of some ideas.
   c. I want to see dresses in person or in online stores first.

6. What must-have is necessary for this shopping experience?
   a. Champagne
   b. Snacks
   c. Music

7. How thorough do you want your dress shopping to be?
   a. I want to exhaust all my options—I don't mind trying on 100-plus gowns.
   b. I'm fine with trying on twenty or so gowns before settling on one.
   c. If I love the first gown I put on, I'm as good as done.

8. What do you want to get out of your dress shopping?
   a. I'd like to get the dress and all of my accessories in one swoop.
   b. I'd like to get the dress and will worry about accessories later.
   c. I'd like to go in without an agenda and see what I find.

9. Whose opinions, besides your own, really matter when shopping for a dress?
   a. My mom's/parents'
   b. My fiancé's
   c. My best friend's

10. What's the most important thing when it comes to choosing a gown?
    a. That I absolutely love it
    b. That it's super unique
    c. That it fits my budget

For the Groom: Your Personal Style

Some see their wedding day as a chance to switch up their style; others want to stay true to who they are day-to-day. Ask yourself these questions to help you get a sense of your overall style as a jumping off point for what you want to wear at your wedding.

1. If you could sum up your everyday style in three words, what would they be?

_____

_____

2. Who are your personal style icons? (Could be people whose style you admire or people whose style you like to emulate.)

_____

_____

3. Are you more apt to wear a blazer and nice shoes or a T-shirt and flip-flops?

_____

_____

4. What's your favorite or go-to outfit and why do you love it?

_____

_____

5. What, to you, makes a great suit or tux? (The color, the fit, the style?)

_____

_____

6. Do you enjoy getting dressed up or look at it as a hassle?

_____

_____

7. Do you want your overall look for your wedding to be similar to your everyday style or would you prefer to do something different or unexpected?

_____

_____

8. Is there anything you feel strongly about wearing, or not wearing, on your wedding day? (Like a vest or cufflinks?)

_____

_____

9. What are your wedding wear priorities? (Comfort, that you coordinate with your partner, that you can wear the suit again?)

_____

_____

10. When you picture yourself on your wedding day, how do you want to look? (Sharp, dapper, relaxed?)

_____

_____

For the Groom: What Should I Wear?

Here are some common styles for groomswear. Use this list to help stylists at menswear stores show you options that match your preferences.

1. Tux -OR- suit?
2. Black -OR- white?
3. . . . -OR- navy -OR- gray -OR- khaki?
4. Long tie -OR- bow tie?
5. Patterned tie -OR- patterned socks?
6. Pocket square -OR- boutonniere?
7. Patent leather shoe -OR- regular leather -OR- sneakers?
8. Patterned -OR- solid shirt?
9. Suspenders -OR- vest -OR- cummerbund?
10. Shaven -OR- scruffy?

How Can We Make Our Attire Meaningful?

Some couples have family or cultural aspects they'd like to incorporate into their wedding fashion. Use this quiz to make sure you don't forget any.

1. Are there any family heirlooms we can incorporate into our wedding-day look, like a watch or piece of jewelry?

   _____

   _____

2. Are there any colors, accessories, etc., that have meaning to us, our culture, or our relationship that we'd like to include?

   _____

   _____

3. What are some special ways we can coordinate our outfits without being too matchy? (For instance, the groom might wear a striped pocket square, while the bride dons a striped ribbon on her bouquet.)

   _____

   _____

4. Are there any accessories we can get engraved to make them extra special—like cufflinks, our rings, a watch, etc.?

   _____

   _____

5. Would you consider wearing or incorporating a piece of your mother's wedding gown, a shirt of your father's or grandfather's, or another clothing item into your overall look? What are some ways we could do this?

   _____

   _____

6. Is there anything special we can carry (or even just put in your pocket) on our wedding day to honor a family member or friend who can't be with us?

_____

_____

7. What are some ideas we have for our something borrowed, blue, old, and new?

_____

_____

8. Are there any aspects of our wedding look that we'd like to hand make or that we'd like a family member or friend to hand make?

_____

_____

9. Are there any places on your gown or suit where you can add a monogram or embroidered words? (Or an opportunity to do so with an accessory?)

_____

_____

10. Would we consider donating our wedding attire to a worthy cause or person after the big day?

_____

_____

What Should Our Bridesmaids Wear?

They'll be alongside you during your big day—think about your attendants' looks so they'll perfectly coordinate with your own.

1. All the same color -OR- shades of one color -OR- different colors?
2. Solid -OR- patterned?
3. Dresses -OR- jumpsuits?
4. All one piece (dresses) -OR- separates (tops and skirts)?
5. Matching attire -OR- mix-and-match dresses?
6. Long -OR- short dresses?
7. Heels -OR- flats?
8. Carry bouquets -OR- wear flower crowns/corsages?
9. Updos -OR- hair down?
10. Statement necklaces -OR- pretty belts?

What Should Our Groomsmen Wear?

Yes, you have to figure out what these guys will wear, too. Here are some ideas to get you started.

1. Tuxes -OR- suits?
2. Long pants -OR- shorts?
3. Long ties -OR- bow ties?
4. Patterned ties -OR- patterned socks?
5. Pocket squares -OR- boutonnieres?
6. Patent leather shoes -OR- regular leather -OR- sneakers?
7. White shirts -OR- colored?
8. Patterned -OR- solid shirts?
9. Suspenders -OR- vests -OR- cummerbunds?
10. Shaven -OR- scruffy?

9

Attendants

Incorporating Pets Into Our Wedding

Use the following list to get ideas for including furry friends into your big day.

- ❑ Take engagement photos with our pet
- ❑ Include our pet in our save the date
- ❑ Take first-look photos with our pet
- ❑ Have our pet serve as ring bearer
- ❑ Carry our pet instead of a bouquet
- ❑ Include our pet as part of a wedding logo we can use on our paper goods
- ❑ Create fun drink coasters with a photo of our pet
- ❑ Order a custom cake topper that includes us and our pet
- ❑ Include photos of us with our pet into a slideshow
- ❑ Create a photo booth backdrop that includes our pet
- ❑ Order cookies that are made to look like our pet for the dessert table
- ❑ Donate to an animal organization in honor of our pet instead of giving out favors

Should We Have Attendants or Not?

While having a bridal party is traditional, it's not mandatory. Use this quiz to determine if asking friends and family members to be bridesmaids and groomsmen is right for your celebration.

1. How important is it to us to have a bridal party and why?

   _____

   _____

2. How important is it to us to have a best man and maid/matron of honor and why?

   _____

   _____

3. How many people are we thinking of having?
   a. Your side: _____
   b. My side: _____

4. Do we want our sides to be equal or is it more about having who we want?

   _____

   _____

5. How can we include other important people in our lives who won't be part of the bridal party?

   _____

   _____

6. How much can we budget for wedding party items like bridesmaid bouquets and gifts?

   _____

   _____

7. What other items or expenses do we want to cover for our attendants?

_____

_____

8. How do we feel about having our attendants pay for their own attire for our big day?

_____

_____

9. What do we want our attendants to do? (Stand up with us, take photos with us, get ready with us?)

_____

_____

10. Can these people do these things without being official attendants?

_____

_____

11. Do we have any concerns about having a bridal party?

_____

_____

12. What are our expectations, goals, and wishes for having a bridal party?

_____

_____

Who Else Do We Want to Include in Our Festivities, and How?

Aside from your bridal party, use these questions to help you include other special people on your big day.

1. Which friends or family members would we like to participate in our wedding day?

   _____

   _____

2. Of these people, are any of them great speakers or people who could tell good stories about us? (If so, consider asking one or two of them to speak at your welcome/rehearsal dinner.)

   _____

   _____

3. Do any of these people have a talent or skill that they could contribute to the wedding? (That is, could they paint a pretty art piece that could serve as your ceremony backdrop or help create your menu?)

   _____

   _____

4. Are any of these people younger (around age seven to twelve) who might be able to pass out programs?

   _____

   _____

5. Could we put one of these people in charge of making sure guests sign the guest book? (Great for tweens/teenagers who are too young to be in the bridal party.)

   _____

   _____

6. Would we like to ask these people to serve as ushers/greeters for our guests? (Ushers can be male or female these days!)

_____

_____

7. Are any of these people older (grandparents, etc.) who could be honored with a boutonniere, corsage, or something special they can wear to show their distinction?

_____

_____

8. Are any of these friends or family members people of faith who might like to help with a religious component, if we plan to have one? (Ideas include facilitating the unity candle ceremony or saying a blessing before your meal.)

_____

_____

9. Are any of these friends or family members musically inclined? (Consider asking them to play music for the ceremony or helping you put together a playlist for your DJ.)

_____

_____

10. Are any of these friends or family members great writers? (Consider asking them to write a poem or something poignant about you two to include in your programs or that can be read during your ceremony.)

_____

_____

Honoring Loved Ones Who Have Passed at Our Wedding

Use the following list to get ideas for celebrating those who cannot be present on your big day.

- ❑ Have a table with candles lit in remembrance
- ❑ Wear something of a loved one as part of our wedding attire
- ❑ Section off a set of seats to leave empty in commemoration
- ❑ Include a mention of those who cannot be present in our program
- ❑ Include a special song, poem, or story in our ceremony
- ❑ Mention loved ones in our ceremony
- ❑ Showcase photos of loved ones in frames or as part of a slideshow
- ❑ Donate to a cause that is special to a loved one in lieu of having favors
- ❑ Offer a toast during our meal to celebrate those who cannot be there
- ❑ Include a special food dish or dessert that reminds us of a loved one
- ❑ Use something a loved one has given us, like toasting glasses, at our reception

10

Photography and Music

The Right Photography Style for Us

Each wedding photographer has his or her own style. Figure out what you want before you start looking for possible vendors.

1. Digital -OR- film?
2. Still photos -OR- photos and video?
3. More posed photos -OR- more candids?
4. Photojournalist style -OR- traditional?
5. Artistic (uniquely styled images) -OR- lifestyle (a mix between styled and candid)?
6. High-fashion inspired (posed like a magazine spread) -OR- documentary (more action shots)?
7. More photos of details and décor -OR- more photos of people?
8. Edited/filtered photos (like what you might see on Instagram) -OR- no filter?
9. Textured process (grainy, like old films) -OR- vintage process (more washed out)?
10. Natural light -OR- professionally lit?

Capturing Our Wedding: What Are Our Photography Goals and Wants?

Photographs are a big part of the lasting memories you'll have from your wedding day. Answer these questions to be sure you know what you want ahead of time.

1. Who do we want to photograph us, a professional or someone who knows us?

   _____

   _____

2. How much time do we ideally want to spend taking photos?

   _____

   _____

3. How much are we willing to spend on photography?

   _____

   _____

4. Would we rather have a ton of photos or fewer, more curated images?

   _____

   _____

5. How comfortable do we each feel in front of the camera?

   _____

   _____

6. Do we want to do an engagement shoot? (Why or why not?)

   _____

   _____

7. How important is it to us that our photographer gets an equal amount of shots of both of us? (Rather than focusing more on the bride.)

_____

_____

8. Do we prefer to hire a photographer who is completely hands-on or someone who will take direction from us?

_____

_____

9. Do we want to focus more on photos of just the two of us or group photos?

_____

_____

10. How long do we ideally want a photographer to shoot? (Start to finish? A couple of hours?)

_____

_____

Must-Have Shots

Choose as many ideas as you want from the following list so you can eventually share them with your photographer—and feel free to add your own! (Your professional will know to get photos of the big moments, like the walk down the aisle, the ceremony, the first dance, and so on. These are important shots, but you want to make sure you get ones that are special to you beyond those traditional photos.)

- ❏ Big group photo of everyone at the wedding
- ❏ Magic-hour photos of the two of us
- ❏ Us with any kids at the wedding
- ❏ Pre-getting-ready fun with our wedding party
- ❏ Generational photos (like great-grandmother, grandmother, mom, you)
- ❏ Designated photos with special people (like a childhood friend, an aunt, etc.)
- ❏ Detail shots: just our shoes, jewelry, and so on
- ❏ Candids of us
- ❏ Candids of us and our wedding party
- ❏ Candids of us and our parents
- ❏ Décor details (especially anything we DIYed)
- ❏ Photos of the food
- ❏ Aerial views of the ceremony and/or reception

What Kind of Music Would Work Best for Our Wedding?

Music—whether soft background melodies or loud dance tunes to rock out to—will help shape your wedding day from start to finish. Ask yourselves these questions to decide your preferences.

1. Which musical option appeals to us most for our ceremony?
   a. Live music (band)
   b. Live music (solo artist)
   c. DJ/recorded music

2. What vibe of music appeals to us most for our ceremony?
   a. Something romantic
   b. Something upbeat
   c. Something eclectic
   d. Something else entirely: _____

3. Which musical option appeals to us most for our cocktail hour?
   a. Live music (band)
   b. Live music (solo artist)
   c. DJ/recorded music

4. What vibe of music appeals to us most for our cocktail hour?
   a. Something jazzy
   b. Something light and not super noticeable
   c. Something to get the party started right away
   d. Something else entirely: _____

5. Which musical option appeals to us most for our reception?
   a. Live music (band)
   b. Live music (solo artist)
   c. DJ/recorded music

6. What vibe of music appeals to us most for our reception?
   a. Something fun to dance to, like '80s pop
   b. Something cool and edgy that people can hang out to
   c. Something whimsical
   d. Something else entirely: _____

7. How hands-on do we want to get with our music?
   a. Create a song list of must-plays and do-not-plays for whomever we hire
   b. Create a set list for whomever we hire
   c. DIY and use a playlist we make ourselves

8. How personal do we want our musical talent to be?
   a. Have friends or family members play all the music
   b. Have someone we know sing or play at some point, then hire the rest
   c. Hire all musicians—stick to the pros

9. How important is music to us for our celebration?
   a. Very important—we want to spend a lot of time thinking about what music should be played when.
   b. Pretty important—we want the music to feel appropriate, but it's not our hugest priority.
   c. Not super important—we'll hire good people and let them take the lead.

10. Overall, what's the most important thing music can bring to our big day?
   a. Create a happy, loving vibe
   b. Get people out of their seats and dancing
   c. Create a chill atmosphere where people can mingle

Our Ideal DJ or Band Leader

Choose the right person to handle your entertainment by checking off the qualities you'd like him or her to have.

- ❑ Range of musical styles and abilities
- ❑ Offers to tailor music to fit our needs
- ❑ Tech-savvy
- ❑ Offers lighting options for the dance floor
- ❑ Quiet personality—will just provide the music
- ❑ Big personality—can act as our reception MC
- ❑ Super passionate about music
- ❑ Will get people out on the dance floor
- ❑ Offers feedback on our song list
- ❑ Willing to play what we ask without offering suggestions

Discovering Our Special Songs

Use this quiz to help determine which songs could be included in your special day.

1. "Our song":

   _____

   _____

2. Version we like most (acoustic, instrumental, covers, etc.):

   _____

   _____

3. Song(s) that remind us of each other:

   _____

   _____

4. Musical styles or artists we've associated with our relationship:

   _____

   _____

5. Musical genre that best fits our relationship:

   _____

   _____

6. Favorite songs about romance or love:

   _____

   _____

7. Songs that remind us of when we first met or started dating:

   _____

   _____

8. Songs we've heard on vacation or that remind us of traveling/fun times we've had together:

_____

_____

9. Songs that remind us of specific places of importance to us (like a college song, a sports team's song, etc.):

_____

_____

10. Songs that always make us happy or make us smile whenever we hear them:

_____

_____

Ideas for Our First Dance

For many couples, the first dance is a magical moment they'll savor their entire lives. Use this quiz to figure out which song should accompany it.

1. Slow song -OR- faster song?
2. Classic song -OR- something more contemporary?
3. Just one song -OR- a medley?
4. Live music -OR- recorded?
5. Choreographed -OR- not?
6. Take dance lessons -OR- go for it with our natural skills?
7. Practice before -OR- just wing it?
8. Serious/romantic -OR- fun/funny?
9. Dance whole song -OR- just part of it?
10. Have parents cut in (to segue into a family dance) -OR- just us dance?
11. More traditional dance -OR- plan for some guests to flash mob at some point?

11

Engagement Parties,
Showers, and Other
Wedding-Related Events

What Kind of Engagement Party Is Ideal for Us?

Engagement parties are popular ways to celebrate right away, especially if you have some lead time before the wedding itself.

1. The timing:
   a. ASAP
   b. A couple of weeks postengagement
   c. A couple of months postengagement

2. The type of party:
   a. Surprise—our friends and family don't know we're engaged.
   b. Semi-surprise—only our close family knows the news.
   c. No surprise—the cat's out of the proverbial bag.

3. The location:
   a. The city in which we live
   b. Where our families live
   c. Destination engagement party

4. The logistics:
   a. Just one that everyone can come to.
   b. We'll celebrate the news with our friends and family separately.
   c. Our families live far from each other, so we'll need to celebrate with both sets of parents independently.

5. The setting:
   a. Family home
   b. Favorite bar
   c. Nice restaurant

6. The people:
   a. Everyone who will be invited to the wedding
   b. Just close family
   c. Our local friends

7. The host:
   a. Our parents
   b. Us
   c. A friend

8. The invitations:
   a. Formal and mailed
   b. Fun Evite or Paperless Post
   c. Casual text or e-mail

9. The food:
   a. Catered
   b. Just drinks
   c. Hosted appetizers or desserts

10. The dress code:
    a. Come as you are
    b. Cocktail
    c. Semiformal

What Kind of Bridal Shower Do You Want?

For some couples, the wedding shower is a special get-together that makes the upcoming wedding seem very real! Ask yourself these questions to be sure yours reflects your priorities and preferences.

1. The timing:
   a. The month of the wedding
   b. A month before the wedding
   c. A couple of months before the wedding

2. The host:
   a. Sibling
   b. Best friend
   c. Me

3. The guest list:
   a. Every woman invited to the wedding
   b. Coed—close family and friends
   c. Just the bridesmaids and close family

4. The location:
   a. My home/parents' home/friend's home
   b. Outdoors in a park
   c. At a restaurant

5. The planning:
   a. I want to be involved every step of the way.
   b. I want to create the guest list; everything else can be a surprise.
   c. I just want to show up.

6. The overall vibe:
   a. Super girly
   b. Casual and fun
   c. Fancy and upscale

7. The itinerary:
   a. Tea, small bites, gifts
   b. Mimosas, mingling, brunch
   c. Interactive activities, ample food and drink, hanging out

8. The attire:
   a. Prim and proper
   b. No set dress code
   c. Pretty but not overdone

9. The must-haves:
   a. Traditional shower games
   b. Time to chat with all of my guests
   c. Signature dessert or cocktail

10. The no-ways:
    a. Traditional shower games
    b. Opening gifts in front of everyone
    c. Men in attendance

For the Groom: What Kind of Bachelor Party Do You Want?

Bachelor parties are a rite of passage for many grooms. How will yours go down?

1. The timing:
   a. The night before the wedding
   b. The month of the wedding
   c. A couple of months before the wedding

2. The host:
   a. Sibling
   b. Best friend
   c. Me

3. The guest list:
   a. Bridal party only
   b. Close friends and family
   c. Just my BFFs

4. The location:
   a. Las Vegas
   b. Denver
   c. New Orleans

5. The planning:
   a. I want to be involved.
   b. I want to choose the location and the guest list; everything else can be a surprise.
   c. I want the whole thing to be a surprise.

6. The financials:
   a. I want to pay for my portion.
   b. I'd like my friends to treat me, but I'll take care of my travel expenses.
   c. I expect my friends to pick up the whole tab.

7. The vibe:
   a. Crazy guy's weekend/last hurrah
   b. Low-key bro time
   c. Outdoorsy male bonding

8. The itinerary:
   a. A mix of chill hanging out and going out
   b. Nice dinners and athletic activities, like watching sports or river rafting
   c. Clubbing, clubbing, and more clubbing

9. The must-haves:
   a. A visit to a strip club
   b. A pool
   c. Golf

10. The no-ways:
   a. Exotic dancers
   b. Being hungover
   c. Going to bed at 10 P.M.

For the Bride: What Kind of Bachelorette Party Do You Want?

Bachelorette parties are a fun way to celebrate with your crew before you get hitched. How will yours go down?

1. The timing:
   a. The night before the wedding
   b. The month of the wedding
   c. A couple of months before the wedding

2. The host:
   a. Sibling
   b. Best friend
   c. Me

3. The guest list:
   a. Bridal party only
   b. Close friends and family
   c. Just my BFFs

4. The location:
   a. Las Vegas
   b. Palm Springs
   c. New York

5. The planning:
   a. I want to be involved.
   b. I want to choose the location and the guest list; everything else can be a surprise.
   c. I want the whole thing to be a surprise.

6. The financials:
   a. I want to pay for my portion.
   b. I'd like my friends to treat me, but I'll take care of my travel expenses.
   c. I expect my friends to pick up the whole tab.

7. The vibe:
   a. Last hurrah/crazy girls' weekend
   b. Fun female bonding time
   c. Getting pampered and relaxing

8. The itinerary:
   a. Spa days and great food
   b. Getting crazy
   c. Winetasting and crafting

9. The outfits:
   a. Funny hats/wigs/costumes
   b. Cute coordinated attire
   c. No special dress code

10. The must-haves:
    a. Bachelorette-themed party accessories
    b. Fun games/dares
    c. Shots

11. The no-ways:
    a. Penis straws
    b. Male strippers
    c. Getting home before midnight

What Kind of Rehearsal Dinner Do We Want?

Rehearsal dinners can bring both sides of your families together or serve as a way to welcome all of your guests if you're hosting a destination affair. Answer these questions to make sure the event incorporates factors that are important to you two.

1. The timing:
   a. Early evening the night before the wedding
   b. Later evening the night before the wedding
   c. Two nights before the wedding

2. The type of party:
   a. Set start and end time
   b. Set start time but open-ended
   c. People can come and go as they please

3. The location:
   a. Outdoors in a park or at the beach
   b. At a restaurant or in a rented space, like a winery
   c. At someone's home

4. The guests:
   a. Immediate family
   b. Family and the wedding party
   c. Everyone invited to the wedding

5. The host(s):
   a. The groom's parents
   b. Both sets of parents
   c. Us

6. The food:
   a. Catered sit-down dinner
   b. Just drinks
   c. Hosted appetizers or desserts

7. The dress code:
   a. Casual
   b. Cocktail
   c. Semiformal

8. The agenda, other than food:
   a. Speeches
   b. Music and/or dancing
   c. Games

9. The invitations:
   a. Formal and mailed by the host
   b. Included with the wedding invites
   c. Information only on our wedding website

10. The vibe and décor:
    a. Should coordinate with the wedding
    b. Should be totally different than the wedding
    c. Should be totally low-key so we can focus on the wedding

What Do We Want to Do the Morning of Our Wedding?

Use this checklist to come up with your ideal wedding day by selecting as many that appeal to you—you can narrow the ideas down later, if needed.

- ❑ Sleep in
- ❑ Have breakfast in bed
- ❑ Do yoga/work out
- ❑ Go for a run/bike ride/hike
- ❑ Hang out with friends
- ❑ Hang out with each other
- ❑ Hang out with our families
- ❑ Have ample time to get ready
- ❑ Have some champagne (or other beverage of choice)
- ❑ Get beautified—a manicure/pedicure, a shave, etc.

The Grand Sendoff

Select the ideas that appeal to you from the following list for how you want to end the festivities, then narrow down to your favorite.

- ❑ Have everyone line up with sparklers while we run through
- ❑ Depart via a cool getaway car
- ❑ Do an outfit change
- ❑ Head to an afterparty with all of our guests
- ❑ Sneak away when the reception ends
- ❑ Have a limo pick us up and whisk us away
- ❑ Spend time chatting with guests until the venue kicks us out
- ❑ Fireworks display
- ❑ Sing a song to our guests
- ❑ Give a thank-you speech to end the night

Afterparty Ideas

Will the guests at your wedding want to keep partying all night long? Think about these options for moving the party elsewhere. Circle any venues that appeal to you.

1. Dive bar
2. Karaoke
3. Roller rink
4. Bowling
5. Late-night food
6. Cigar bar
7. Hang out in the hotel suite
8. Night swimming
9. Local concert or see live music
10. Speakeasy-type bar

What Do We Want to Do on Our Wedding Night?

Use this quiz as a jumping-off point to discuss your expectations for the ideal wedding night. Check off as many items as you'd like to accomplish, postnuptials.

- ❑ Open gifts/cards and count the money we get
- ☑ Order room service
- ❑ Check out all the photos on social media tagged with our wedding hashtag
- ☑ Hang out with friends and family as long as possible until we pass out
- ☑ Get busy, *wink-wink*
- ☑ Drink champagne together
- ❑ Eat leftover wedding cake
- ☑ Sneak into the hotel pool for a late-night swim/hot tub
- ☑ Take a selfie of us still in our wedding attire
- ❑ Go to sleep ASAP—we'll be exhausted

What Kind of Morning-After Brunch Do We Want?

Some couples host a morning-after-the-wedding brunch. It can be a fun way to recap the big day, look over photos on people's phones, and say goodbye to those who are heading home.

1. The timing:
   a. Starts at 8 A.M.
   b. Starts at 10 A.M. *)11:00am*
   c. Starts at noon

2. The type of party:
   a. Set start and end time
   b. Set start time but open-ended
   c. People can come as go as they please *(circled)*

3. The location:
   a. Hotel restaurant or by the pool *— Stellas?*
   b. At a nearby restaurant
   c. At someone's home

4. The guests:
   a. Immediate family
   b. Family, wedding party, and anyone who traveled to the wedding
   c. Everyone invited to the wedding *(circled)*

5. The host(s):
   a. Our parents
   b. Us *(circled)*
   c. Another family member

6. The food:
   a. Full brunch buffet *(circled)*
   b. Continental breakfast *(circled)*
   c. Muffins and mimosas

7. The dress code:
   a. Super casual
   b. Pajama party
   c. Sundresses/khakis

8. The invitations:
   a. Formal and mailed by the host
   b. Included with the wedding invites
   c. Information only on our wedding website

9. The guest expectations:
   a. We expect most people to sleep in instead.
   b. We expect mostly older people to show up.
   c. We expect everyone to be there.

10. The other options:
    a. Postwedding beach day
    b. Afternoon pizza party
    c. Skip next-day activities entirely

12

The Honeymoon

Where Should We Honeymoon?
(Domestic)

Planning to stay in the United States? Here are some popular honeymoon destinations. Circle any you'd like to consider.

1. Maui
2. Napa Valley
3. Jackson Hole
4. Palm Springs
5. Yosemite
6. Sedona
7. Cape Cod
8. Ashville
9. Aspen
10. Austin
11. Chicago
12. Key West
13. Nashville
14. Savannah
15. Santa Fe
16. Juneau
17. Big Sky
18. Miami
19. Las Vegas
20. San Francisco
21. Orlando
22. Lanai
23. Washington D.C.
24. Hilton Head Island
25. Santa Barbara

Where Should We Honeymoon?
(International)

Have passport, will travel? Circle some possible destinations for your honeymoon. Circle any you'd like to look into further.

1. Tahiti
2. Italy
3. Iceland
4. Belize
5. Scotland
6. The Maldives
7. Japan
8. Australia
9. South Africa
10. France
11. Thailand
12. Peru
13. Spain
14. Morocco
15. Greece
16. The Virgin Islands
17. Fiji
18. Indonesia
19. Ireland
20. Germany
21. China
22. The Galapagos
23. Aruba
24. Russia
25. Panama
26. The Cayman Islands
27. Namibia

What Kind of Honeymoon
Do We Want?

From short, local getaways to weeks-long extravaganzas, honeymoons come in all shapes and sizes. Use this quiz to narrow down your options.

1. The timing:
   a. Right after the wedding
   b. A week after the wedding
   c. A month after the wedding

2. The travel:
   a. Somewhere we can drive to
   b. Somewhere we can fly to under four hours
   c. Somewhere farther away than four hours by plane

3. The itinerary:
   a. Stay in one city or place the whole time
   b. Travel around one area or region
   c. Go to multiple cities or countries

4. The type of vacation:
   a. All-inclusive resort or trip
   b. Cruise
   c. Book everything ourselves individually

5. The locale:
   a. Beach/tropical resort
   b. City
   c. Nature/mountains

6. The planning:
   a. You're planning it.
   b. I'm planning it.
   c. We'll plan it together.

7. The accommodations:
   a. Go all out and stay in a hotel suite/nicest room available
   b. Book a bed and breakfast
   c. Stay in a vacation rental

8. The agenda:
   a. Lots of lounging and relaxing
   b. Sightseeing and exploring
   c. Being active, from hiking to biking

9. The priorities:
   a. Romance
   b. Great food
   c. Adventure

10. The duration:
    a. A long weekend
    b. A week to ten days
    c. Two weeks or longer

End-of-Book Wedding-Planning Wrap-Up Quiz

Whew! You've covered a lot in these pages. Think about these questions as you wind down the conceptualizing part of the wedding-planning process.

1. What has been the most surprising part about wedding planning?

   _____

   _____

2. How has planning brought us closer together?

   _____

   _____

3. What strengths has our planning revealed (in ourselves and our relationship)?

   _____

   _____

4. What challenges has our planning revealed (in ourselves and our relationship)?

   _____

   _____

5. How has our relationship grown over the course of planning?

   _____

   _____

6. What have we learned about each other while planning?

   _____

   _____

7. What have we learned about ourselves?

_____

_____

8. What have we fought about most while planning?

_____

_____

9. What have we agreed upon most?

_____

_____

10. How has our overall wedding vision changed since we started this journey?

_____

_____

11. How have we made planning fun for each other?

_____

_____

12. What compromises did we each have to make while planning?

_____

_____

13. Are there any decisions we've made that we wish we could change?

_____

_____

14. What are we most looking forward to about our wedding?

_____

_____